Live a Better Life

Earning Passive Income Online

By Nathalie Marran

About copying and sharing this Book.

Copyright Nathalie Beulah Marran 2018

The rights of this book ARE NOT transferrable upon purchase.
That being said, sleepless nights and long, long days have gone into the creation of this book. Even with the occasional bout of procrastination, it is still a collection of my efforts. Don't be that person who passes it on, gives it away or copies it for free, or worse, sells it without knowledge or permission of myself, the author.

This book is dedicated to my wonderful wife who is my biggest fan and my greatest support system, always there to cheer me on through the good times and the bad. I count myself incredibly blessed to have her in my life.

Index

In the Beginning
What is passive income?
What is a digital product?
Getting rid of distractions
Who are your clients
    Create repeat clients
    Marketing on Social Media
    Become Social Media Savvy
How to get paid
For Writers
    Amazon.com for Writers
    Lulu.com
    Smashwords.com
Crafters and artists
    Handmade on Etsy
    Case Study: Vee's Knits
    Make money with YouTube
Photographers and graphic designers
    Shutterstock
    Case Study: MarranArt
Musicians and filmmakers
    Createspace
Create a multi-layered product
In Conclusion

Bonus eBook
Blogging – The Basic Money Maker
    Index:
    Introduction
    My Personal Story
    Setting Up
    Affiliate Programs
    Become an influencer
    Sell your own products
    Blog Set Up Check List

In the Beginning

The beginning is the most important part of any work ~ Plato

Are you a writer? Artist? Graphic artist? All round creative spirit? Ever wondered how you could embrace your skills to help you to create a passive income for yourself? In this book I am going to take you through a variety of online marketplaces and platforms that you can use to help you to create a passive income and have a financially free future. I will also offer you various other tips and tricks to help you along the way.

Many great business minds of today believe that poverty can be eliminated by people beginning to learn how to earn even just a basic salary from online sources. I truly believe that this is possible, not only that but I have made it my goal to show people EXACTLY HOW they can go about achieving just that!

These are practical, usable solutions. Start today, **invest in yourself**, and your tomorrow will be so much brighter, but to get there, start today! That's the first, and most important step.

In my twenties I worked in a small company, I worked hard and was quickly elevated to a position where I controlled the day to day running of the business. Although my boss then made a lot of mistakes as far as working with his employees went, he also had a lot of good qualities too, and ideals he tried to instil into our minds.

One of these was the importance of passive income, and learning to generate a decent passive income for ourselves. It was well over a decade ago, and the internet wasn't quite what it is now, but over the past few years a lot has happened, to the point that, if you know where to go and what to do, you can really invest in your own skills, generate content, and most importantly start earning a fairly decent passive income.

All those years ago, when I started investing and looking for ways to generate passive income in my twenties, the options were pretty limited, such as investing in shares, purchasing property, writing a book and submitting it to a publisher to hopefully get published, etc. The world has changed phenomenally since then, and a lot of huge strides have been made, especially over the past five years, where creating a passive income no longer requires a lot of capital outlay, but rather just your time and skills.

I want to start by mentioning that I'm not an "overnight" success story, and I'm a bit too old to be a millennial who is trying to publish some thumb sucked information in order to get a few of your dollars... nope, this book has been about five years in the making. That's right, I'm going to share with you what I have learned over the past FIVE YEARS, of investing time and effort in myself and my work, that has allowed me to truly start to generate a decent passive income, simply by creating digital products for online use. I'm going to go through the various platforms that I have used and share with you my personal experiences and tips, so that you too can work towards achieving your personal goals of earning an income from the world wide web.

In fact, I have made it one of my aspirations to be able to research as many of these platforms as possible, covering a wide variety of products and services. In this book I am going to cover the biggest and easiest ones to help you to get started, however if you follow me on Patreon, every week I will be covering a different platform or service that you can use to help you to get well on your way to earning a passive income online.

Visit me at
https://www.patreon.com/itsmybusiness
and invest in yourself and your future!

Does this work? Can you learn to earn passive income from online sources? Yes, absolutely, however like any asset base it takes time to build up and get there, but if you are willing to put in the work then read on, because this may just be the book to help you to start on the path to become financially free.

I'm a serial entrepreneur and artist. However I make the majority of my earnings through passive income, and not just any passive income, but passive income through online, digital products.

The videos I create on Patreon, and the information in this book are ideally suited to artists, writers, photographers, musicians and creative people in general, **but anyone who is interested in creating digital products to sell online will definitely find my videos and book useful and helpful.**

My personal story; for my day to day work I am a sewing pattern designer, and the founder of Sew You! Magazine. Naturally I don't want to work until I'm a hundred years old, because I have to, if I work, it should be because I want to. Five years ago my journey of creating online passive income started for me when I sold my very first digital sewing pattern. A whole new world opened up for me, and I never looked back.

After pushing myself with growing my business for a number of years, I had a big "failure" which knocked me really hard. As an entrepreneur, I've had a good few of these, and I've always found a way to come out of it bigger and stronger than before. This particular time, I really struggled to get myself back together, and for three months I spiralled into quite a dark depression, and it would take another three months for me to be fully back up on my feet. So in the middle of this, when I had really hit the bottom, what was it that made me get up, dust myself off and get going again?

Well I realised that even though I was in a dark place, and I had shut down mentally from exhaustion, and I felt like I just couldn't... even with all of this going on within myself, the money kept coming in.

Let me say that again... the money kept coming in, even though I wasn't really working. I had thought that my business and my plans were in a bad state, but they weren't, it was nothing that could not be fixed. And I had successfully built myself up to the point where my income was passive – I really did not have to work to have money coming into my bank account.

This got me excited, and inspired to keep on moving forward, and now things are even better than before. I have even started helping with coaching others, so that they too can learn to do the same.

Ask yourself this question: Right now, can you take a three month break from doing any work at all, and will your income still flow into your bank account?

If you wish to retire, or stop working, do you have enough income coming in to sustain your current lifestyle?

If not, then this is a really great place to start. By reading my book, you should be able to find at least one avenue that you can use that will help you to start earning a passive income in the very near future.

As a life coach, and a passive income specialist I have worked one on one with my clients to help them to grow and understand their product base, as well as themselves. You are your own brand, and growing your brand (you) is just as important as growing your passive income.

As a result, I developed a series of lifestyle techniques to help my clients to develop themselves as well. I will share some with you in this book, and I will share a good few more through my videos.

To watch them sign up at
www.patreon.com/itsmybusiness
and **invest in yourself!**

What is passive income?

This is a topic that I felt is very essential to cover first. Not only will it help you to understand it better, but you will have a better understanding of what is required of you to generate your own.

Ideally passive income is made from you having to do work *once off* to generate a product. Once you have completed the work, you can continue to make money from that product with no further work required, or at the very least a very minimal amount of work.

But a little more on that in a bit, first I want to cover a few tips with you...

Before we get started, I highly recommend that you have pen and paper handy to make notes while you read my book. I am supplying you with a lot of information that you may want to refer back to. So when you feel you need to, or you really want to remember something that I mention, stop and make your notes.

Researchers have also proven that if you write something down, you are much more likely to remember and use that information.

For those of you who love to be as organised as I do, you can download and print a folder and note pages that I custom designed for you to use, this way you will be able to refer back to your notes quickly and easily. The folder set is available in my Etsy store, www.etsy.com/shop/marranart - I have a good few stationery items available to assist small business owners and creators.

Tip: Studies have proven that if while reading and learning something new, if you read a word that you do not understand, your brain actively stops learning, simply because you read a word you did not know the meaning of. If you find yourself reading down a page, but you suddenly realise you have no idea what you just read, and you feel that you haven't absorbed any of it, then go back and see if perhaps there was a word or phrase you had passed that you did not fully understand.

Keep a dictionary handy, and if you wish, write down any word you did not understand and its meaning (according to the context). It's a really great way to ensure that you absorb as much of the information as possible that I am sharing with you.

*

So what is passive income really? Let me break it down for you.

The word "passive" means, roughly translated "no work required" or "no effort". required". In truth there is no such thing as truly passive income, there will always be some work required.

For example, rental properties are a great source of "passive income", you buy the property, rent it out, and money comes in. However you are still required to do some work, for example, making sure your rental agency ensures you have a tenant and that they pay you, and that your book keeper takes care of all the paperwork and figures thereafter. It's very little work, but there is some work involved, and usually it's the kind of very little work that nobody minds doing at all.

The word "income" – well I don't think this one really needs much explanation, it simply means "money coming in".

So "Passive Income" means: Little to no work or effort for money to come in.

So what is digital passive income? Now this is my absolute favourite part. In the physical world, your quantities are limited. By this I mean, a company only has so many shares to buy or sell, you can only sell a product according to the amount of physical inventory that you have available to you, your services offered are limited to the amount of hours in your day, your rental properties can only have one tenant at a time. Although all of these forms of income are wonderful, you are limited.

If you create a digital product to sell online, firstly, once the product is created and is ready to sell, you don't have to re-create the product every time you receive a new client placing an order. The product is already complete. However, most importantly, it's a digital product, which means once you have created it, it can literally be sold an *infinite* amount of times.

I want you to take a moment and think about that. If you create a really great digital product to sell, once it has been created there is absolutely no limit to the amount of times that you can sell it. There is no pressure for capital outlay to invest in a large amount of stock, that will sit in a storeroom or shop somewhere, with the hopes that it will sell. In fact with most of these processes I will share with you, the only cost you will have, is quite simply, your time.

That's right, you can create a passive income with no money down, just your time. And we all have time, right?

But, and here's a BIG BUT - you actually have to want to achieve this. I share this information with a lot of people, especially people that I believe can truly benefit from learning how to earn a passive digital income. 9.9 out of 10 times I can actually see that it goes in one ear, runs through "the filter of a million excuses" and out the other ear.

I believe this is because I'm not offering a "quick fix" or an instant solution to many people's financial problems. The sad truth is that "quick fix" solutions don't work, except for the person who is offering them, because they got your money. Instead I'm offering a way for you to look at growing your income *over* the long term and *for* the long term. Those same people who don't take my advice are quite often in the same position five years down the line, where those who do take the time to learn how to earn their passive digital income, find themselves in a very different position. One that is more empowering to them and their circumstances.

So why is passive income important? Well, ask yourself these questions;
Do you want to work your entire life for money to cover your month to month expenses?
How will you earn your money if you retire, or find yourself without employment?

Can you really save enough money to be able to live a really amazing, adventure filled life should you decide to stop working?

Perhaps it's time to start making some changes, and investments in *yourself* so that your future can begin to change.

And the best part is, that everybody everywhere has *at least one skill* that they can turn into a digital product and sell online.

What is a digital product?

What is a digital product? Well it's exactly what it says, it's a product created digitally on your computer, and sold as a digital file. It can be a pdf document, or a graphic image you have created, it can be an mp3 of a song you wrote, an mp4 of a video, or a digital book, eBook, photograph, etc.

It requires no stock levels or capital (money) tied up in those stock levels, which you hope will sell so that you can at least make your money back. It is literally a type of file, that when broken down to its core is made up of ones and zeros, and can be sold an **infinite** amount of times.

The only real rule to abide by here, is that it must be your own creation. Something you came up with from the depths of your imagination, and created digitally using a program on your computer or electronic device.

This new digital product revolution is giving creative people all around the world the power to create their own income. From artists to musicians, the software available to us today allows us to turn our own homes into recording, art and even filming studios. I believe that it is at the point now that those who love to write, sing, paint, and create can write their own pay cheques and possibly even earn more money than more traditional high income careers. I believe that you just need to know where to look, what communities to join, and to find the right platform (or two or three) to launch your products on.

In this book I am going to cover several of the more well known platforms to help you to launch your own online income stream, and as long as you're willing to put the work in to create the products, opportunities will open up for you.

But before we get started on the platforms, I want to cover a few things to help you on your way. These tips will help you to create your products, find your clients and get you well on your way to success.

Getting rid of distractions

Most of you who will be reading my book will be creative people and artists, and let's face it, the one thing we are really, really good at is finding ways to procrastinate and delay the creative process that will allow us to create our digital products in the first place.

In order to be able to successfully push past the obstacles that cause us to procrastinate, we have to be really disciplined with ourselves, and set time aside especially for our creative endeavours.

Actively set time aside, and stick to it, don't let anything or anyone take away from this time you set out for yourself.

Take out your diary and specifically set aside at least an hour a day (yes every day, how badly do you want to earn passive income and be financially free?). Let your family and loved ones know that this is your creative time and that they cannot disturb you. You have to take this seriously, otherwise they won't, so make sure that they are fully aware that this is something that you are incredibly serious about.

Plan your week in advance. Put aside time at the end of every week to plan your time for the next week. *Remember goals are just dreams that you have given a deadline.* If you want your dreams to come true, make it a goal, and diarise time to work towards it.

Switch off your phone and any electronic devices that are not necessary for your creative process. You cannot have random emails or whatsapp messages interfering with your process, they will quite literally just cause unnecessary distractions.

DO NOT GO ONTO ANY SOCIAL MEDIA PLATFORMS AT ALL! There is not a single status update in the world that is more important than you growing your future. If it is at all possible, don't be on the internet at all. This is your time to be completely focused on your task ahead.

Plan your time. Before you start your creative time, already know what it is that you are going to be doing during this time. If you enter your creative hour without a plan, you might find yourself just staring off into blank space for an hour instead of getting anything done.

If you are going to be writing, have an idea of what you are going to be writing about, and how many words you expect to write during that time. If you are going to be creating a new digital graphic, have an idea of what you are creating first, find something that inspires the image of your task ahead. If you need to create a mood board before you start each project, then do so. A mood board is a really great way to help keep you focused on what it is that you want to accomplish from your specific creative project.

Most importantly, take action and just do it! You will find that there are days when it's hard to create your digital products, just do it anyway, work on it. There will be days when you produce terrible and unusable work. At least you did something, which is better than most people will ever do, even if you don't sell it, you will be investing your time in creating a really important habit. By making creating a habit, and a part of your every day way of being, you are quite literally investing in your future.

The truth is, if you just start and work on your projects every day, you will get better. Your skills will improve so much so that one day you will be able to look back and see the huge improvement that you made. By starting and working on your passive income projects every day, you will, like me, one day find that they are paying for themselves and you can take a break.

By just starting and staying focused, you will do more than most people ever will. Staying focused is a huge key to your future success, don't let things like television or Facebook become your excuse.

Poor excuses lead to a poor future.

Something that I have done that I have found to be incredibly helpful, is that I make tech free times and days a habit. I don't go onto any of my devices for a couple hours before bed time, and I try to stay away from them before 10am (at least) in the morning. Doing this alone has given me a huge amount of time in my day, I'm able to be focused and get tasks done much more quickly and effectively.

Then I have taken this process one step further. Once a week, I have a completely tech free day. A day where I stay away from all my devices, and stay off of the internet and any form of social media platforms whatsoever, and guess what? These tech free days usually turn out to be my most productive.

Without distraction I could easily write up to ten thousand words in a day. That means that if I kept to it, I could complete a book in ten days, or less! (Ever wonder how Barbara Cartland could write so many romance novels in a single year? I doubt she let herself get distracted).

Going on your phone and devices also fills your brain with "information overload". You see, you might actively only pay attention to one or two images, or a few status updates, but your eyes are seeing everything, and your brain is subconsciously taking in everything that you see on the screen, even though you are not aware of it. What this does is it triggers a level of anxiety, and you may find yourself feeling overwhelmed by even the simplest tasks.

It is however quite a vicious circle. A lot of people who feel overwhelmed usually go onto social media, sometimes just to distract themselves at the task at hand, for "just a few minutes" so that they can take a break before continuing, not realising that on a certain level, they are actually increasing their anxiety levels.

Other times, we go onto social media to post a status update, or a photo... or to Instagram that lunch time salad, to show just how good you have been. When your peers acknowledge your post with a "like" or a comment, you actually have a sense of accomplishment.

Unfortunately it's a *false sense of accomplishment*. To put it in really simple terms: what you did was you completed a task, all on your own, and then you were acknowledged for doing just that. The acknowledgement was your reward, and you felt as if you actually accomplished something. However in reality, you did not.

So with this false sense of accomplishment, along with a heightened level of anxiety from the over stimulation of your brain, you now return to the actual task you had at hand that you had to complete. The result is that you feel overwhelmed and frustrated that you can't complete your work, and that you just can't "*get this done*". So feeling frustrated and overwhelmed by your work, or the task you had set for yourself, and feeling that you can't complete it, what do you do? You guessed it, you turn back to social media again where you can be validated for being awesome.

In a nutshell this explains why social media is so addictive, and why it can result in a lot of people "living online" instead of accomplishing tasks and being present in the "real world".

However social media isn't all bad, just for those days when you want to be creative. Once you have completed your products however, social media may just be the best way to help you to reach your clients.

Who are your clients

Believe it or not, as an investor in your own time and skills to develop products to sell online, you are an entrepreneur, you are a business person, and you are creating your own business, whether it is full time or part time. You are investing in creating and growing a brand, and that brand is you, and your skills or what you are able to offer the world is your product.

This also means that you need to approach creating your products, as a business owner would, and there are a few essential questions you need to ask yourself, and a few processes to go through before you start.

Take out your notebook or notepad, and write down each of the following questions, and under each question, I want you to give an answer with as much detail as possible.

Do you have a product that will sell? Why do you think so?

Who are your clients?

What need does your product(s) fulfil? – List up to three reasons why people would want to buy your products.

How do you reach your clients?

Where, online, are you most likely to find them?

Are you passionate about your product or service?

Do you have fun generating new content?

Most importantly, what motivates you? What are your reasons for doing what you are doing? If you don't have a powerful enough reason, then you don't have a strong enough driving force to motivate you to continue what it is that you are doing.

When it comes to discovering what your driving force is, make sure that it's something that you are truly emotionally passionate about. If you do not feel a lot of passion and excitement for the *reason* that you are doing something, then it may be time to reconsider it, to find a new reason, or even a completely new approach.

As you would with any business venture, take some time and complete a SWOT analysis. Write down your **S**trengths, **W**eaknesses, **O**pportunities and **T**hreats.

Understanding this will help you to know where to start, and on which areas you should work more on and pay more attention too.

Before you even begin, it will be incredibly useful to know what it is that you are doing, and why it is that you are doing it.

Once you are well on your way however, and you have your first few clients in and you start earning that income, you will want to change your focus on bringing those clients back and to be able to sell new products to them. You already know that they love your product, let them know when you have new ones that they can be interested in.

Create repeat clients

Repeat clients are one of your greatest assets, and can make up the majority of your income. First of all, having really great products that they enjoy in the first place would be the best place to start. Once you have their attention and interest in your products, you can then focus on bringing them back for more.

Be consistent. Once you begin to grow your client base, and you gain more and more loyal clients and followers, being consistent in delivering new work can be a huge drawing card. For example; if you stick to the cycle of posting a new product every second Monday, then your biggest followers will eagerly be awaiting your new product every second Monday. Being consistent allows clients to really become fans of your work. And they will not only tell others about your products, but when and where they can get them too.

Create excitement, if you have the time. People love dealing with people. If you can find a way to share your creation process with your clients (usually on social media), not only will they eagerly follow you during the process, but they are also more likely to invest in the final product, as they feel that they have really been involved in the creation process.

I have a photographer friend online, who always shares little stories and snapshots of what she's getting up to during a photo shoot. As a result I always find myself eagerly awaiting images of her final product. And I know that I'm not the only one, she literally has hundreds of people who follow her for the same reason. She builds up excitement before releasing those final images, which are usually amazing and beautiful.

She has successfully used this process to also gain paying clients for her photographs and digital product offerings

Once someone has purchased one of your products, encourage them to sign up for an email newsletter. If they loved your product, they will probably do just that.

This is a really powerful tool to have in your arsenal for creating a great digital passive income, and it is one of those times when just doing a little work can pay off in a big way. The art of creating loyal return clients can be summed up in pretty much two words... "email newsletter".

Yes it absolutely requires some work from your side. If you are not sure of how your time schedule looks, then dedicate to only writing monthly email newsletters. If you find that you get more time along the way, then consider moving onto weekly newsletters (which has been proven to be the most successful for gaining repeat clients). You will also want to be careful to not repeat yourself too much, or bore your followers, as this is a sure way of losing them. If you don't have enough "meat" for the content for weekly newsletters, then rather stick to the safety of a monthly email newsletter.

Your newsletter should be updates on what you are getting up to, and any new exciting product releases that you might have. With every marketplace and product range that I cover in this book, I recommend adding links or details for your clients to be able to sign up for a newsletter. If they do, then you know that you will easily be able to market your products to those clients who are already interested in them. This is the main reason why email newsletters have the highest conversion rates out of any type of marketing.

I highly recommend using Mailchimp. Visit www.mailchimp.com – it's free to sign up, and they have a pretty decent free option for those who are just starting to build up their newsletter base. They have a great assortment of tools and systems in place to help you to create really effective campaigns – from pre-designed templates, to guides on how to get your clients to sign up to your newsletters. You can even link them to social media posts and run Facebook ads from your mailchimp interface. If you are short on time, Mailchimp allows you to create a number of newsletters and schedule them to only go out on a specific day at a specific time. They also offer you research tools that help you to work out what types of newsletters work best for your brand.

***Get my monthly email newsletter - Packed with all the latest news on my upcoming videos and book launches!
http://eepurl.com/dGCcu5***

There is a reason why they are one of the world's leading sites when it comes to email marketing, and this is always the first site that I recommend to anyone who is looking at using an email platform of any kind, to bring back return business.

Marketing on Social Media

Love or hate social media, it's the number one source of where you are going to find your clients to buy your products. Different platforms allow you to reach a wide variety of clients in different ways, and without a doubt you will want to be on as many of these platforms as possible.

Posting onto the various social media platforms can become a really time consuming process, valuable time that you can use to generate more content and digital products online which can result in more income coming in, the catch is though that there will be no income coming in if you don't share all your goodies with clients and possible clients across social media platforms.

What you need is one single site, where you can post from and all your posts are broadcast across the various social media platforms, saving you a lot of time that you would have wasted going onto each platform individually and posting from there.

Hootsuite (www.hootsuite.com) is by far the best in the business when it comes to this. They reach the widest variety of social media platforms, and have an array of social media posting services that will make your life so much easier.

You can schedule posts months in advance (though I recommend only scheduling one month at a time), you can also automatically set up Hootsuite to post across the social media platforms at times when it feels that you are more likely to reach your highest traffic flow. They have a "built in" algorithm that works out when the best time will be for you according the social media platform you are posting to as well the country you are based in.

You also have an option to set specific times for specific posts to go live. If you really so wished, you could spend one afternoon a month setting up all your posts, and then sit back and relax, and work on doing what you are good at while the app does all the work for you.

The downside is that Hootsuite only offers a free 30 day trial, after which it becomes a service you need to continue paying for.

They are the best at what they do, and it shows, but you will need to decide if it's an investment worth the cost. I used Hootsuite for two years before I decided to move on, my main reason for moving on and trying other products available was, firstly to see what other platforms were offering, and secondly to find if there was a single platform that offered a similar, FREE service.

A tried a good few platforms, none of which particularly impressed me (it's hard when you move on from the best, to try out the rest), but then I eventually came across a site that ticked a good few of the boxes.

Buffer (www.buffer.com) has a really decent free service, as well as a paid service which has a whole host of extras at usually a similar cost to Hootsuite. If you are looking for a free platform to post to social media with, then this is the place where you will want to start.

The free service on Buffer is quite limiting though. They don't post to as wide a variety of platforms as Hootsuite does, and you can only choose to link your free Buffer account to three social media accounts. You would need to decide which are your three strongest platforms, and stick to posting on those (any others you will have to post onto yourself).

Although you can choose regular time intervals to post to social media, buffer doesn't automatically pick the best times for you, so you will need to see during which times you are able to reach the highest traffic levels, and then set Buffer to post at those times, and you have the option to add posts at specific times as well, in case you have one day when you need to change a time slot.

The biggest down side though to Buffer's free version, is that you can only schedule up to ten posts per platform at a time.

In a way this works out quite well for you, after all you don't want to be constantly bombarding your social media followers with information, one or two posts a day is usually more than sufficient, especially if you make sure that they are effective and impactful posts. This means that should you choose to make two posts a day, you can schedule your posts up to five days in advance, or if you decide to only post once per day, you can schedule your posts for up to a week or even ten days in advance.

This means that at least once per week, you would need to set time aside to set up your posts for the week. It's still well worth it and way better than making time to go onto social media every day, which leads to, usually, a lot of procrastinating and way too many distractions.

Buffer's paid for version allows you to add more social media accounts, and set up more posts in advance, but their free service is a pretty great place to start.

One of the things I really like most about Buffer is that every week they email you a "Social Media Report Card", which is really helpful for seeing how your social media posts are doing, and if what you are doing is working.

It tells you how many people your posts reach, gives you a breakdown on the interactions you have had, and tells you which of your hash tags were the most effective. Using this data supplied will help you to improve your posts, and ultimately reach a wider audience for your products.

Become Social Media Savvy

Calm down, calm down! This isn't so tough. In fact, I've put together a few tips for you to help you to better share creations across the various social media platforms, get interaction from followers, and of course to generate a few sales.

Tip #1: Don't Sell! Sell! Sell! People actually hate being "sold to" on social media platforms. This is where you will be **informing** your possible clients, not "selling" to them. If you want to mention a product, tell them something about your product that they didn't know, like what is its best feature? What can it be used for? etc (not the price).

Tip #2: Be human – people like to do business with people, not companies. If your followers like you and feel that you are more a friend that they follow, rather than a business, they are more likely to pay attention to what you have to say... and sell.

Tip #3: You're selling a lifestyle (especially effective on Instagram) – your followers are following you because you like the same things, it's that simple. You like to sew / write / crochet/ paint / invest, etc... and so do they.

Show them how you incorporate these things into your daily life - take a holiday picture of yourself knitting on the beach, show them the new fabric you just bought and can't wait to make something out of, look how you can jump up and down in these new pants you just created... sell the lifestyle, and you will sell the products too.

Tip #4: Ask Questions! That's right, ask your followers questions that they will want to answer. To make it even better, both Facebook and Twitter offer polling options, where you can create a poll with selected answers. Make it fun and quirky, but also use it as a great way to generate some market research

Your followers are following you because, as I have mentioned, they have the same interests as you. This also means that they may be doing something very similar to what you are doing. Ask them to share details about their latest projects, ask them what they get up to during the day, asking them for their opinions on certain things.

By involving your followers in this way, you are making them feel special and important, and as if they really matter to you. Even though it may be a pre-scheduled post (not that they need to know that), if your followers feel that you are giving them attention and acknowledgement you will be creating a connection which will create loyalty. Simply put, people like to be made to feel special, and to be around people who make them feel special.

Tip #5: Use pictures, great pictures sell. Pictures sell more than words ever could, so learn to use just a few words in your descriptions but post effective pictures that will sell your products. Don't add words to your pictures where possible, it has been proven that images that contain a lot of words are often ignored by social media users.

Tip #6: Include all of your social media details on your products, where you can. People are buying your products because they love your work – let them know where they can find you on social media so that they can see more of what you have to offer.

Include them in video tutorials, or in the actual digital files of the products. If you're writing a book, include all your social media links at the end of the book. Include them wherever you can, so your followers know where to find you.

Tip #7: Don't abuse HashTags... in fact research has shown that the use of more than THREE HashTags often lowers peoples interactions with your posts, and it kind of scares them off.

So use at least one relevant hashtag, for your post and one, maybe two others at the most. The only exception to this rule is Instagram... which is fuelled by hashtags. Instagram allows you to include up to 30 hashtags per post, where possible try to use up all thirty.

If you're not sure which hashtags to use, then I highly recommend using the site Top HashTags (https://top-hashtags.com) they will help you to find and discover the top hashtags that will work for you and your products.

The rule to follow when it comes to social media, is that you want to make posts with the biggest impact, have the widest reach, but at the same time you want to use the least amount of time to do so.

Your goal here is to generate a passive income, although some do use paid marketing through various social media platforms, I personally don't recommend it.

I have tried paid advertising on most of the social media platforms, but unless you are a large company or have a large budget, the only thing you will more than likely achieve though paid advertising is, getting yourself into debt early on in your business. That is something that you want to avoid altogether, the goal here is to earn a profit, not run at a loss.

The best way to get the greatest reach is through really impactful posts that people love and share, and these types of posts are seldom paid for, and are often free. Why not do a little research on your competition (those selling similar products) and see which of their posts had the most responses, this will give you an idea on the approach that you can take for similar results.

How to get paid

Once you have products, and you know how to reach your clients, you will want to make sure that you have access to your hard earned money.

Before you even get started with launching on the various websites, it is really important to know how you will be receiving your money. The easiest way, on most of these platforms, especially if you live in a non-major territory (country), is to open a PayPal account first.

PayPal (www.paypal.com) makes receiving your money (and of course earning in dollars) so much easier. So unless I specifically stipulate it in any of the details of the various platforms, this is the way that you will most likely be paid. So take your time to set up your PayPal account, and to set up how you will be withdrawing your funds from your account.

For example, here in South Africa you can only draw your money out of PayPal, via an FNB (First National Bank) account. However they have made the process rather easy, all you need to do is set up an online banking profile and link your PayPal to your existing bank account, with any South African bank.

It's essential to do this first, as PayPal has a strict regulation that you need to withdraw your funds from your PayPal account within than 30 days of receiving it. I imagine this is one of their terms and conditions for many countries, so put in the effort and make sure that you are fully set up before you get started with selling.

Once you are ready to receive your monies, then it's time to start looking at which platforms you will be selling on.

For Writers

Amazon.com for Writers

I am going to jump right into it and start with possibly one of the biggest sites, that we all know, and love or hate Amazon.com, if you learn to work well with the site you can really earn a decent income stream from it.

You can use amazon.com for several different reasons, from selling your own products, drop shipping, to selling digital products, such as magazines, books and music, to joining their affiliate program. Amazon has really worked hard at putting their fingers in as many pies as possible.

Even with all of this going on, let's face it Amazon is best known for their books above all else, and it is their KDP self-publishing service that will earn you the most passive income, and for that reason, it is the area that I am going to focus on for the purpose of this book.

Amazon has done a very remarkable thing, they have been at the forefront of digital technology and have completely changed the publishing world, or at the very least had a huge influence in those changes.

To start you would put your blood, sweat and tears into crafting a book. As any author knows, it's as if you take a piece of your soul, your very existence and put in black and white on paper.

Traditionally, you would then submit your manuscript to publishers, "selling your soul" so to speak, in the hopes that they would actually publish you. As a writer myself, I know the pain of receiving rejection letter after rejection letter. It was a tough, scary, and a somewhat horrible experience, and still is for most writers.

Then on 19 November 2007, Amazon launched it's very first kindle (which sold out in 5 hours) and the digital book revolution really started to take off. Suddenly Amazon was offering a digital platform where writers could self publish their books without all the hassle and agony of having to deal with an actual publisher, or having to fork out the upfront costs involved with having to self publish a limited run of your book (and then still having to try find somewhere to sell your newly minted pages). Now anybody from almost anywhere in the world could publish, for free, and all it would take was the time and effort involved in the actual writing process.

Magazines and newspapers the world over were sharing articles, pondering if this new digital book revolution would be the end for the printed page. Especially now that Amazon makes the entire process easy and streamlined.

Amazon even has their own ISBN system set up, so that, as long as you're selling on their platform, you don't have to go through the efforts of registering your own ISBN. You however will still need to do so if you wish to sell your books on any other platforms.

Even with all this "digital book" excitement, Amazon had to admit that nothing beats holding an actual book in your hands.

In 2016 they took the self publishing scene to a whole new level, now allowing their authors to publish paperback copies of their books through their "print-on-demand" service. What this means is that self published authors on Amazon can now sell their digital books in a paperback option, which Amazon has printed and shipped, one at a time, every time a reader orders a copy, at no additional expense to the author.

Becoming a successfully self published author could not be any easier. All you have to do now, is put in the effort that is required to actually write a book.

Have you ever wanted to be the next Stephen King in the horror genre, or Barbara Cartland in the Romance genre... wanted to write your own fantasy or science fiction novel? Well here is your chance. I'm going to break it down to you in very simple terms.

The actual writing process is up to you, there are literally thousands of books, software, courses and sites out there that will help you to work out how to create your novel, and create great characters. That's not what this book is about. I'm going to tell you what is required of you to be able to actually complete your book and sell it, the writing process is purely up to you.

I have however created a stationery toolkit to help you during the writing process. **Visit www.etsy.com/shop/marranart** *to view it. It's a folder to help you keep everything together, pages to write on, and also includes 30 cards with writing prompts to help you on your way, and to help you through any writer's block.*

Firstly I recommend writing **at least** 80,000 to 100,000 words for a decent size novel or book. To start, let's be safe, and stick with 80,000 words. If you put your mind to it, it is usually fairly easy to write a thousand words in about an hour or two.

So let's say you currently have a tough full time job to pay all the bills. When you come home, instead of flopping down in front of the couch to mindlessly watch the television box, why not first write 1000 words. You can always reward yourself with television afterwards.

This would mean that after 80 days you would roughly have 80,000 words. Say realistically you only end up writing 20 out of 30 days in a month. This means that it will take you four to five months to write your book, if you are doing so part time, (does not seem like much after all).

Take another month or two to proof read, re-read (and please also get a friend or two to do so too if possible), and let's say at a push within seven to ten months you have a brand new shiny novel which you can self publish.

Going onto Amazon and creating an account as a publisher is incredibly easy. Their interface is really user friendly and easy to follow. They will even help you to set up your book for paperback publishing, and have a variety of book cover options to choose from if you don't already have one.

They have also recently set up a system where you can order a printed proof-reading sample and have it shipped to yourself. You will be amazed at the errors your mind skips over from when you are reading on a computer screen to when you are reading black ink on white paper.

They also offer you the option to order *author copies*. This service allows you to order several copies of your books, directly from Amazon, at cost price. This is a really fantastic idea if you find that you are able to host a workshop, where your book will be a beneficial add on, or if you are able to attend events, markets or expos where you will be able to reach possible readers who would be able to immediately purchase your book.

A really fun way to use this feature is by ordering books and hosting a local book launch and book signing session, and invite your local fans to come and meet you, and friends and family to come and support you.

Tip: For writer's in non-major countries, Amazon.com will want to send you cheques instead of paying into your bank account, which can offer certain difficulties. I would recommend going onto www.payoneer.com and setting up an account with them. This makes receiving payments from Amazon so much more easy, and you don't have to wait to reach the $100 dollar limit, they will pay you every month, even if you've only earned just a few cents.

Amazon will take their share of the profits before paying any royalties over to you, however it will be much less than the huge chunk you would lose if you went through the traditional publishing system.

Did you know that traditionally published authors only receive about 10% royalties from the sale of their books, that's if it's a hardback edition – for paperback an author only typically receives 8%. If you self publish through Amazon, your royalties are 35% to 70% from the sale price (depending on the territory the book was sold in) a HUGE difference.

What is KDP Select and why should you sign up for it?

Amazon Kindle Unlimited members can choose to "lend" a book a month at no cost, and with no return date - sort of like the best library ever, and this is really beneficial to you as the writer. When you publish your book on Amazon, you have the choice to select adding your book to the Lending Library, I highly recommend that you do, and here is why.

Every month, out of the Prime Membership fees, Amazon puts together a large bonus amount, usually a couple million dollars.

For every page of your book that is read, you will receive a small portion of this fund. Because there are literally hundreds of thousands of books an Amazon, it usually only works out to be a couple of cents per month, however, it is better than nothing at all.

There are two other even bigger advantages to the lending library. Firstly, if enough people read through the first ten pages of your book, your rating on Amazon goes up, and your book is more likely to be recommended to even more readers, which boosts your sales. However, I have found that the biggest advantage by far is, that quite often someone will read the first few pages of your digital book, and if they love what they have read, they will then pop online and purchase the paperback version. This actually happens more frequently than you would think, and translates to not only a brand new book sale, but you also get paid for the pages that were read from the borrowed digital version of your book.

Do you need any more reasons to love the idea of self publishing on Amazon? Well here's a tip – keep an eye out on their new "Audible" label for audio books – it may just be possible in the near future to add your very own audio version of your book, a great way to attract new readers and followers of your brand.

Why **NaNoWriMo**? And what is it? If you are truly serious about "one day" becoming the author you have always wanted to be, then why not this year take up the NaNoWriMo challenge.

NaNoWriMo stands for **National Novel Writing Month**. Every year, in November, thousands of authors from around the world attempt to write a 50,000 (or more) word manuscript between the 1st of November and the 30th of November. Is it possible? Absolutely! You would only need to average 1667 words per day (just today I have already written more than double that, and after working hours too).

It is a really great way to get yourself committed to finally beginning that writing career that you have always wanted. To make it official, you can sign up and pledge your pages at www.nanowrimo.org – will this be your year? If not, when will you begin?

I don't, however, think it's necessary to make it official. Every November I set aside time to complete the task of a writing project, I however just make sure that I dedicate the time to getting it done, without sharing it with everyone – and I usually do. I do it this way so that I don't feel overwhelmed about having to stick to an official commitment, which for me personally is counterproductive, though I know that some people are more likely to complete the task if they do make it "official". The preference is up to you.

It is possible to begin to earn a really great side income from self publishing on Amazon. Dedicated writers who really work out a great writing system in their genre (all you need is a great plan and standardised novel layout), can publish up to two books a year if they are doing this part time. Once you have loyal readers lined up, they will eagerly await your next title.

Create an author page, it's a must! Amazon gives all of its authors an "about" page where you can introduce yourself to your readers, and let them know a little about who you are. Writers with author pages have statistically proven to be a little more successful at selling their books than those who don't.

> *Tip: Arts and crafts books are also hugely popular, even if you are not an author or novelist, but instead you love creating handmade products, why not put a book together on your craft, with lots of practical activities, for others to enjoy too. This can be a really great complementary platform if you are already using another platform to sell your goodies on, such as Etsy.*

Lulu.com

At first glance Lulu (**www.lulu.com**) *has it all* for the self publisher who is looking to earn a fairly decent passive income.

From Lulu's platform you can sell on Lulu, Amazon**, Barnes and Noble** and iBookstore, plus a few other marketplaces, making it much easier for you to reach a much wider audience, and they offer coupons and discounts for you to share with your readers to help boost your book sales.

When you sign up they even supply you with a free eBook: *Author's Guide to Success - A Complete Plan for Publishing and Selling Your Book.* Which will help you to understand everything that is required for you to be a successfully published author on Lulu. You will also receive weekly emails packed with tips and advice to help you on your way.

Every day around 1,000 new titles are published on this site, and they offer authors all the assistance they need to make sure their books are of top quality, they will even support you with all the formal issues, like assisting you in registering an ISBN (for USA residents only). Like Amazon however, they offer the service of allowing you to use one of their custom generated ISBN numbers, for use when selling books through their platform, and associated platforms, however if you want to "go it your own" on a different platform, using books published through Lulu, you will have to register and apply for your own ISBN and globalREACH distribution package.

They also offer the service of having your book printed as a paperback, and for those who are interested, **they have hardcover options too!**

Unlike Amazon though, Lulu prefers that you purchase a proof copy of your book first to approve before launching your book for sale across various platforms, in fact you can't advance in the publishing process until you have ordered and proof read a copy of your book.

They also take 6 to 8 weeks to launch your printed book, where Amazon usually takes no more than three days.

This has been acclaimed as the best website to go to for self-publishing, and I can see why. It allows you to publish your book in eBook and printed version. It has a wide array of tutorials to help publishers, and also a list of professional services which self-publishers can use to make sure their books are of the best quality.

They are much more intense about the entire publishing process, making sure that you stick to strict guidelines, so much so that you would possibly get quite nervous throughout the process. However, all of this is in place to make sure that you are only publishing the best quality work, which is what you want to achieve in order to create bestselling books.

The entire process is well worth it, and every step along the way actually helps you to become a better author. You have already put in a lot of effort to create the best book or novel that you could create, why not make sure it's of the best quality.

To print and sell your eBook, costs you nothing up front, and is a great way to start.

This site also has a little something for photographers and artists. It has a layout to help you to create calendars to sell, featuring your own artwork.

Oh and did I mention, they give you the option to pitch your book to Hollywood representatives... yes, they really do! You do however need to be able to make your way to the United States to be able to take advantage of this option. But they will train and coach you before you meet with the Hollywood execs to make sure that you give your best possible pitch!

When it comes to publishing printed versions, you can absolutely do so on Lulu, you just need to be able to buy your proof copy for approval first, unlike Amazon who make it much easier for you to set up your book for "Print on demand" without paying anything towards it.

Lulu's process is a much lengthier one, but when you have the time and budget I do recommend giving it a try. In the meantime though, I recommend getting started on Amazon.

You can choose to sell solely on Lulu, as they do offer the service of selling your books for you on Amazon in kindle format, though I find that it makes more "passive income sense" to publish separately on Amazon and Lulu in order to fully take advantage of Amazon's print on demand service.

Like Amazon, who offers you an author page, Lulu also offers you an "author spotlight" page, free of charge. Again I recommend taking advantage of this and claiming your page as your readers are more likely to purchase your books if they know more about you.

You will need to spend a fair amount of time on Lulu.com, getting to know your way around the publishing process.

The website is packed with information and references, and services to help you become an amazing author. So do take the time and have a good look around.

One thing that I can promise you is that it is well worth it.

Smashwords.com

Smashwords launched their site with the spirit of rebellion. Their goal was to go against the norm, and allow writers to be able to self publish their works. They have been around for ten years, having launched in 2008, and regard themselves as the biggest Indie publishing site.

They offer you a lot of tools and resources to help you to become the best author that you can be, including a podcast from Mark Coker the co-founder, on how be a Smart Author. Visit their a "about" page to give it a listen.

They supply you with a lot of tips and tools, and are also honest with you about what you can expect from the site as far as book sales go. Like Amazon and Lulu, they also assist you with a free ISBN, to be used for only selling on their platform and not any other.

Their interface is the simplest and, I found, the most user friendly so far, and allows for the speediest publishing process. You don't have to do any waiting, your book is quite literally up for sale immediately after you have uploaded it.

However, it is important to know, that even though your book is already available for purchase, Smashwords will still review your book, and they will pull it off their digital shelves if they feel that your book, especially its formatting, are not up to standard.

Unlike Amazon and Lulu, you are required to design your own book cover, and they don't supply you with any tools to create an option through their site... but that's really a small hurdle that we can easily jump over.

When you sign up to the site, they recommend you download (for free) the *Smashwords Style Guide* eBook by Mark Coker, to help you to create the best version of your eBook before jumping right into publishing it. I highly recommend that you download and read this book, as well as go through the "about" page which is packed full of extremely useful information.

They only publish eBooks, and don't offer printed versions, however, I absolutely love this site as it already allows you to record and launch your very own audio books through Findaway Voices.

They go through the process of producing the audio book for you to ensure you only have the best quality available. You assist in all the steps, and even get to interview your own narrators, and they launch and sell the books for you on a variety of platforms.

It does come at a cost though. Once you start the process of producing an audio book, Findaway will submit a quote to you for the costs, and you can decide to go ahead with it or not at this point.

As with anything when it comes to earning passive income, unless you really have the extra cash laying around, rather save up your earnings to cover the costs of your audio book production, you should never have to "put yourself out" at the beginning. The benefits you pay for should be ad-ons that you can afford once you know you are doing well enough to be able to afford them.

Crafters and artists

Handmade on Etsy

Etsy is possibly the biggest most successful platform available to us to be able to sell our "handmade with love" products on. They are the biggest platform for artisans to sell handmade and vintage products, from all across the world, and may become one of your best sources of creating passive income. Currently, Etsy is my biggest source of passive income by far.

Why do I say that? Etsy has a large enough traffic flow through their site, so much so that I don't actually have to do any active marketing for my products. I don't have to do a thing, other than creating my products and posting them, to get people to find them and buy them – though additional active marketing does help to boost my sales, email marketing in particular.

So how does a "handmade" product translate into passive income? Don't be fooled by the "old school" way of thought when it comes to the concept of handmade. I think when we hear the word, we automatically think about the hours it takes to handcraft an item, which we then work at selling. You are right, it does take hours to craft beautiful products to sell on Etsy... but that does not mean that it can't be a digital product.

Some examples of handcrafted products sold on Etsy are, digital images such as photographs. Ready to print stationery, such as wedding invitations. Digital patterns and guides for sewing, knitting, crochet, embroidery, etc. I'm sure that you are starting to get the idea.

As long as it is something that you have created out of your own, you can sell it on this platform. The Etsy marketplace also has one tool that many other online marketplaces don't necessarily have, that really gives it a strong stand when it comes to digital products, and that is that buyers can download the products immediately once they have purchased them. This also means that once you have uploaded your products to sell on Etsy, little to no work is required from you thereafter, and you can begin to sell your digital products an infinite amount of times.

A side note: If your digital products are patterns for sewing, knitting, crochet or cross stitch, you might also want to check out the following site: www.craftsy.com – it doesn't generate as much sales as Etsy, but it offers a similar service.

Etsy has recently increased its costs, which negatively impacted the income of a lot of handmade artisans. I recently heard complaints from a number of people that due to this that they would no longer consider selling on this marketplace.

It did impact most people, especially with products with low prices, but it would have impacted "made to order" stores the most, or stores with actual physical stock, that someone is sitting with. But if you are creating really great digital products, that you can sell as many times as you wish, then even though your profit margin is a little lower than it would have been a few years ago, you will still be earning an income from doing next to nothing.

Don't let an excuse like this deter you from building something that will help you to grow your future income. It really is a case of "every bit counts", and big or small, profit is profit, and what you will be earning from Etsy, after paying your monthly fees, is quite literally pure profit, with no extra work necessary.

Etsy buyers and sellers have a huge base on social media. There seems to be more Facebook and Google+ groups and pages dedicated to this marketplace than any other. Not only do a lot of these pages offer marketing assistance, by way of sharing products and store links to the thousands who are on these pages, but they are also offering you a very focused way of being able to reach your possible clients. People who don't sell on Etsy, but who join these groups are usually looking for unique "handmade with love" gift ideas.

Another tool a lot if these groups take advantage of, is that of hosting "Twitter Parties", or similar events across various social media platforms.

A "Twitter Party" is when a group of people with similar interests make posts on twitter, during a set time frame, and they share the tweets of others doing the same. You can join in on these parties, and follow them by using a specific hashtag. For example, Etsy store owners all go online for a specific hour every day, and they share links to products in their stores, and they share the links that other Etsy store members are sharing too, and all the posts contain the same hashtag, to indicate that they are taking part in the event.

It is a really great way to get to know other store owners, to network with entrepreneurs with similar interests, and to extend your market reach and grow your client base. Most of these parties are moderated and have rules, so make sure you find out what they are before joining in.

Before posting on Etsy, or any marketplace for that matter, first have a look around at what others who are offering similar products are doing with their stores. This will help you to get an idea of what kind of stores are more successful, what pricing to consider, and more importantly, it will give you a really good idea of what the competition is doing, and you can see if there is a niche that isn't being fulfilled that perhaps you can specialise in.

Case Study: Vee's Knits

As a way of helping you to translate how you can take the information that I am sharing with you, and use it to begin to generate a passive income, I'm going to from time to time share a case study with you. Below is the first one, and I hope that it really gives you some great ideas of where to begin.

Vee is almost sixty years old. She is a semi-retired mother of four who spends all her free time training to run the Comrades Marathon, one of her lifelong goals.

Vee is hoping to learn to earn some passive income to make her retirement more comfortable. But she does not know where to start.

She has a laptop, and some experience on the workings of this modern internet thing but she's not sure how to go about building up digital products to earn an income. Some of her favourite pastimes include knitting and crochet, with the occasional bit of embroidery.

I had a discussion with Vee about taking her evening time hobbies, and turning them into a source of income. How so? Well, in the evenings Vee sits in front of the television and usually has a knitting or crochet project to keep her hands busy while she does so, and most of the time she is making up the design as she goes along. As it turns out, a good few years ago she used to have her own knitwear business, so she really has an in-depth understanding in this area of thread craft.

So now Vee has a product, she knows how to design knitting patterns. It's something she already does for herself in her free time, so why not keep a record of what she is doing and create knitting patterns that she can sell online.

Once she has completed a knitting project, and recorded all of the steps along the way, she can take photos with her phone, and write down the pattern and save it as a pdf on her computer. All she needs now is a platform to sell her patterns on.

Her best platform to start selling on is Etsy, where she creates an online store and can upload the pattern details and files, and leave her patterns to sell while she concentrates on her daily Comrades Marathon training.

Her second option, is to set up a store on the lesser known platform *Craftsy*. Craftsy is absolutely ideal for her, they love knitwear projects, and their website is focused on all those who live to knit, crochet, quilt and sew. It is also absolutely free for her to sign up and sell her patterns. Craftsy believes in supporting indie designers like Vee, who use their designs as their main source of income, so they charge absolutely no fees and all the income generated goes to the designers.

Craftsy has a smaller traffic flow to Etsy, but it's a great place to start. Etsy charges a $0.20 fee for every product loaded or renewed on their site. They also charge a 3.5% transaction fee, and on top of that they charge taxes relevant to the country you live in. Vee lives in South Africa, so Etsy charges 15% VAT on top of their fees. The up side however with regards to Etsy is that there is a higher traffic flow, made up of people who generally have a love for handmade crafts, so her chances of making more sales are significantly higher, and her fees are only payable at the end of the month, giving her a little breathing room.

Like Etsy, Vee can load all her files onto Craftsy and little to no further work is required while she continues with her Comrades training.

Two other sites Vee can consider are:

Our Village – a very new marketplace. Like Etsy and Craftsy, Vee can load her digital products and leave them to sell. However their $5 monthly fee, payable at the beginning of the month, is currently a bit much for her, so she wants to wait a few months, until her patterns are selling enough to be able to cover this fee.

When it comes to earning passive income, you will want to pay as little money as possible out of pocket. The idea is to have your products pay for themselves. If the sales from your digital products don't yet cover certain expenses, then you want to consider not taking on those expenses until you are able to do so.

The fourth site Vee can consider is HelloPretty.co.za, this is a South African marketplace for South African artisans. They have an option to sell without a monthly fee, but for higher sales commissions, or you can pay a small monthly fee, and HelloPretty takes a smaller piece of your pie when you make a sale.

To start, Vee will take the first option, she might pay a higher commission to HelloPretty, but that's only if she makes a sale. If she doesn't make any sales at all, it literally costs her nothing to have her products up for sale on the website.

HelloPretty does not allow Vee to upload digital files onto their site. Vee has to mention in her product description that it is a digital file, and when she receives an email confirming a sale, she needs to go and actively email the client, and update the order progress manually on the website. Because this requires a little extra work, and Vee doesn't always have the time to follow up on her emails while she is busy training for the Comrades Marathon, this is a site she will consider only after she has completed her race, and has a little more time on her hands.

By the way, if you would love to take on a new knitting project, pop into Vee's online store to view the products she has available:
https://www.etsy.com/shop/veesknits

Once she has over 100 patterns recorded, Vee can consider compiling a collection of her patterns, and putting them into a book form. Once the book is ready, she can self-publish it an Amazon.com. Amazon has recently upgraded a lot of its features to allow for good quality colour images in their digital books for Kindle. Vee can also choose the option to have her book available as a paperback, available to purchase through Amazon.com.

Once she has more time on her hands, she can also compile a book on the very basics of knitting. How to get started for the beginner, throw in a few tips and tricks, and even a couple of easy patterns to follow.

If she plans well, this means that within two to three years Vee can easily have over 100 patterns for sale, plus two books successfully published, and a Comrades Marathon Medal. She would also begin earning a small supplementary passive income. She can look at the work that she has done, and decide what is working well and what isn't, and expand her brand from there. After five years, who knows where she could be and the type of income she could possibly be earning.

She could even start to record videos of her knitting patterns, and she could create a channel on YouTube where she could earn even more money.

But that's all future plans, for now she's just really happy that she's making enough money and can buy herself brand new running shoes with her first batch of earnings.

Make money with YouTube

We all love YouTube, it's wide array of channels has without a doubt got something for everyone, even if it's just to feed an addiction of watching funny cat videos.

There's even a channel where a guy makes bowls... yes bowls, out of an assortment of materials, he uses something different in every video, and people love watching him make his bowls. I wouldn't say he has any particularly impressive skills, and his processes are almost always the same, he's not particularly funny or entertaining either. Yet he has thousands of followers, thousands of people who watch him making his bowls. So if you ever think that you don't have anything to share on YouTube... just give that a thought.

YouTube is a really fantastic way that you can use to make money, directly or indirectly, by sharing your videos with the world. This is one of the platforms where being consistent really pays dividends.

Make sure you post your videos regularly, on the same days at around the same time, your followers will want to know exactly when they can watch the next episode on their favourite channel.

Firstly, let's look at how you would go about indirectly earning money from YouTube.

This is for when you create videos that are tutorials for clients, that revolve around an existing product that needs to be purchased. For example if you create digital sewing patterns, the video would be a sew-along for how to go about cutting and sewing according to an existing sewing pattern that your clients would need to go purchase. They purchase the product, but the video tutorial is for free.

You can also show videos on how you go about creating certain products, again the video is free, but the completed product is available for any of the viewers to go to your online store and purchase.

You can also create a video on how to use, or the various uses for an already existing product. This kind of video works really well for stores who are looking at drop shipping. You purchase a sample of one of the products you will be selling on your site, and create a video on how to use it, a modern take on an infomercial if you will, but without all the nasty "call now" numbers flashing on the screen.

To sum it up, the videos are free to watch, but the clients are encourage to purchase the product being represented in the videos.

Another option is, in the description of your videos, to leave links where viewers can click through to make a purchase, or sign up for a subscription (a lot of Patreon users use this technique). You can also leave your PayPal details if you would like someone to make a direct donation to you for your efforts – this is used mostly by people who are offering advice, or giving a service for "free" via their YouTube channels. For example, if in your videos you are offering a "realistic" experience through your videos, such as a first person point of view video, or an ASMR video, where you are actually offering an *experience*, leaving details for your followers to "tip" you via PayPal can be quite beneficial.

So how do you make money directly through YouTube?

This is a little more difficult to achieve, but with time, patience and perseverance, it can definitely be done.

I'm sure that you know all of those annoying little adverts that pop up while you view a YouTube video? Well the person who's video it is, they are getting paid for that advertising space.

That's right, the videos are free, but the creators are getting paid by selling ad space. So how do you go about doing this.

Firstly, you need at least 1,000 followers on your channel, and you have to have a couple thousand viewing hours within a month, every month, to qualify. YouTube won't even let you pick your own channel url until you have at least 100 followers.

This is their way of making sure, that simply put, you are not wasting their time, or the time of the paying advertisers. They want to know that when an advert is launched that it absolutely will reach its intended audience.

Yes, you might post one or two videos and become a huge overnight sensation, loved and adored by millions, while YouTube throws money at you, but realistically to earn an income from YouTube videos you are looking at posting in the region of up to 100 videos before the figures can really come rolling in.

Only a small handful of your videos will attract the largest group of viewers, but as of yet, you don't know what type of videos that may be. So get started. If you manage to post a video per week (which is not always that easy, so plan your time carefully), then you are looking at up to 52 videos a year, which means that within two years YouTube could be paying you.

More realistically though, consider posting once every two weeks, to once a month. It does mean that it could take up to four years before you can start seeing the profits, but at least you started somewhere, and that's the important part.

If you never start, you will never get to the part when you begin to earn money.

Photographers and graphic designers

Although for the most part photographers and graphic artists can share their work on sites like Etsy, where clients can download digital prints, or putting together a book or album, or even a calendar, of your best works through platforms such as Lulu and Amazon, what I really want to focus on here are sites especially focused on artists and graphic designers.

Shutterstock

I think, let's start with the most obvious site, Shutterstock. Amongst all of the sites that specialise in selling licensed photographs and graphic images, Shutterstock is by far the easiest one to get published on.

They're not too worried about things like the subject of your images, all they really check is that your images are of a good, useable quality. It is up to the artist to ensure that their work is sellable.

You can load hundreds of "pretty" pictures, and never sell a single one. Shutterstock doesn't care about your levels of creativity or your expressions as an artist, and quite honestly neither do the clients of the site.

If you want to really sell on a site like this, or any photography and graphics sites for that matter, you need to be able to create work that is usable.

The main client base of these sites are marketing departments and agencies. What they are looking for are generalised images that they can place branding on for marketing purposes.

I'm sure that you have all seen those adverts of a person standing, seemingly thinking.... usually the model is standing against a blank background, appearing to be pondering something, and a thought bubble emerges from the model to indicate the reason for such deep pondering.

Most agencies and marketing departments just don't have the budget to hire a professional photographer, model and makeup artist just for the purpose of creating such a simple image. Instead they turn to sites like Shutterstock where hundreds of photographers already have similar images for them to choose from, at a fraction of the cost.

This is the kind of photograph you need to consider selling. It may not be your best artistic creations, but it is what sells. When you take photographs for these types of sites, ask yourself if it would be useable in a marketing campaign.

My best all time selling photograph on Shutterstock is one that I took of my little Jack Russell when she had ringworm. Who would buy such an image? Well pharmaceutical companies to veterinarians the world over, quite literally. It's an image that was easily usable for marketing materials.

One of the most common images you will find, are those of desktops, counter tops, table tops, etc, usually with a few items pushed aside, and a huge open space.

You should really do a bit of homework, and research what kind of images sell best, if you want to make passive income this way, you will have to "go with the flow" and do what everybody else is doing. Shutterstock does help with this, they often let you know what the seasonal trends are, and what types of images your should start posting in order to get sales in the near future, so definitely follow them for this useful information.

Artists, graphic artists and photographers are probably top on the list for those who will find it easiest to earn an income from online sales. Shutterstock is just one of the options, you can also create ready to download work and sell it on online marketplaces like Etsy and Our Village, and take a piece of the pie that crafters have (your digital work is your craft after all), but there are also loads of sites that you can sell on that especially focus on your skills.

One of the top sites is Creative Works (www.creativeworks.com). This is a HUGE marketplace for you to sign up to and sell an array of digital products, from stationery such as business cards, brochures, etc to digital stationery, fonts, logos and photography as well. They specialise in selling digital works of art – but that can be used practically.

However, before you approach this site to sell on, have a look at the sellers who are already on the platform, and how they market their products. You will notice the extremely high quality level of work available, that is because Creative Works only accepts the best work and artists for their site. If you have really top level work, then this is the site you will want to be on, above all the others. There is an application process to go through in order to qualify to sell on this site, so make sure that you are set up and ready to go.

However, if you are still working on honing those graphics skills. there is another site worth looking at. Before this site was uniquely valuable only for those with mad coding skills who wanted to make a few extra dollars on the side, but recently they upped their game and started to add the skills of graphic designers. It looks like they are aiming to add similar skill sets to that of Creative Works, but because they are brand new to the market, they are not terribly strict about the quality of work that they sell through their site.

So if you are a pretty good graphic designer, but you are still working on your skill, however in the meantime you would like to get your work out there and selling, then have a look at the website Adsella (www.adsella.com) – they may still be small, but I think in the future they are really going to be making their mark, so why not sign up now and get in on the "ground floor" so to speak.

The best part, it's absolutely free, and really easy to get started.

Case Study: MarranArt

This is actually one of my own brands that I developed in order to expand my existing skill set, and to be able to be featured on a much wider variety of platforms.

I have been working on graphics programs since my early twenties, I am completely self taught. I have the ability to look at and understand computer programs fairly quickly and easily, so it wasn't a very difficult thing for me to do. Ten years later, in my thirties, I decided to finally complete a graphic design course and get my official certification.

My actual work is designing sewing patterns, which I do pretty much every day using graphics programs, but every now and then I like to break out and do something different. I also have a side hobby, and love for photography. I can spend hours behind a camera taking an assortment of pictures, then a good few more hours in front of the computer editing those images.

I love pushing myself to discover and attempt new things and to see what effects, etc that I can create. In 2017, I finally decided to add this to my skill set, and why not create a range of digital products while I develop my graphics skills even further.

To start, for any graphics designer who is serious about having a career in this field, it is absolutely essential that you consider launching your own website which will showcase your graphic design skills.

Even if you are not looking at doing this as a part time business, or as a means for creating passive income, there will be numerous companies that will specifically ask to see your online portfolio if you apply for a job with them, so go ahead and create your own website.

Wordpress (www.wordpress.com) is going to be one of your best options to consider. They offer a free version that allows you to use several templates to easily set up your own domain. It is an incredibly easy user interface to follow, and they also supply handy tutorials if you are feeling a little lost or need help. You do have the option to purchase your own domain name, if you wish to do so, but a free domain works just as well for this purpose.

The biggest bonus of signing up to Wordpress, and getting to know the interface rather well, is that you can actually add this to your list of skills on your resume, as a lot of companies work through this site, which is why I would recommend this site above any of the others.

I chose my custom Wordpress url https://nathaliemarran.wordpress.com and got busy setting it up. Every time I feel that my skills get better, I make sure to update my website (which is usually fairly frequently).

Anyone who visits your website will be visiting with the intention of seeing your best work, so make sure you always have your latest work up and put your best foot forward. It's not necessary to blog regularly on this site, especially if you are not big on blogging. However for some, by regularly posting blogs on your personal sites, that share information of how well you actually know the areas that you specialise in, you will often be much more "attractive" to future employers or clients, so it is something to consider including.

If you are creating graphic products to sell online, this site can become an invaluable tool for you. Websites such as Creative Works and Adsella will ask you for your custom domain so that possible clients can go and have a look at the quality of your work before deciding to purchase your product or work with you. As a graphic designer, launching and maintaining your own website can be a really huge investment in yourself.

On my website I included all of the details of the various areas that I specialise in, including links where necessary, such as links to my Shutterstock portfolio.

I also created an Etsy store, where I can sell my custom designed stationery (https://www.etsy.com/shop/marranart), and linked that to my website. I put a lot of work and effort into my photography and designs, and want to reach my clients through as many platforms as possible. (I also launched on OurVillage.com and HelloPretty.co.za).

Another website I launched my product range on was Gumroad (www.gumroad.com) It's a site dedicated to creative people who want to sell their digital products online, however it is not a marketplace where people go to buy these products, so how does Gumroad work?

If you launch your own website, or blog, it is often required that you upgrade to a paid version (an example of this is Wordpress), where only once you have a paid plan can you monetize your site. Gumroad has a beginner's package that's free of charge, and allows you to use their site as a backend, to load your products to sell directly on your own website, via the use of embedded html code.

Once you have loaded your products onto Gumroad, you then copy the html code for that product, paste it onto your website, and just like that you have a free back end and check out process to sell your products directly to your clients. Pretty handy right? And you didn't even have to upgrade to that paid version!

So if like me, on your website you are showcasing digital products that your clients can download immediately once they have purchased it, this is how it will work. You add the html code to your website's product page, your clients click on the link to purchase immediately, they then "check out" via Gumroad, where you have also uploaded the digital files. Once payment is approved, they can then download the files.

This is a free service that can really help you as you begin to launch your very own digital brand, and be able to sell products online. There is a paid plan on Gumroad as well, but it will only be necessary to look at this function if your business takes off. The paid plan gives you more storage space and allows more features than the free plan, but once again, the free plan is perfect for you if you're just starting out.

Now Adsella also offers the same service as Gumroad, once you have loaded your product onto their marketplace, they supply you with an html code to embed onto you own website (remember that part where I mentioned that Adsella was first for coders).

The biggest bonus with Adsella is that because they are a marketplace, there is a bigger chance for you to make more sales, and there's no limit to the storage space that you can use. In a way, they pay you to use their site for the same reason you would pay Gumroad to use theirs.

Deciding which site to go with (if not both) is up to you, do your homework and go visit each site and decide which one you would prefer to go with.

These are just a few platforms for you to begin using, and they are really a great place to start to launch your digital product range on.

Musicians and filmmakers

Createspace

There is one site I felt should definitely be mentioned in this book, and although I'm focusing this section specifically on musicians and filmmakers, it really is a site than can be widely used by almost anyone.

Createspace (www.createspace.com) is a subsidiary of Amazon.com, and it really is a basic platform that you can use to launch yourself onto the passive income earning podium.

It is a publishing "back end" that you can use to successfully create products, which are then sold on Amazon.

You can launch an album directly as a CD, and sell it on Amazon. You will need to supply the tracks, all the details of the tracks, and all the artwork for the CD and CD inserts, make sure you have everything ready before you begin.

The product is then sold on Amazon, but only "burned" and shipped "on demand". So your album is ready and sitting and waiting for your fans to purchase it.

Or perhaps you have a gig, and would like to have a few CD's handy, have a few printed and sent to yourself, ready to sell at any event.

This product is also really great if you have your own audio files you wish to sell, such as podcasts, or any audio recording. Why not launch a CD? Are you a stand up comedian? Here's a great platform to get a few CD's out to listeners who can appreciate your sense of humour.

The second product that Createsapce helps you to create and sell online, are DVDs. This is a really great opportunity for break out filmmakers, to launch their movies and shorts directly onto the Amazon platform. Perhaps you are an animation artist, and have a few animations you have created and would like to try your hand at selling.

This is also a really great product for anyone who wants to sell classes, as long as the filming quality is fairly decent, why not give it a try.

Whatever your trade may be, ask yourself, is there a series of classes that you can film that you believe that others will greatly benefit from? Why not record a few classes and create the DVD's. If you're attending an event, why not order a few that you can sell or hand out to your fans and followers.

Are you an exercise instructor? Here's a great opportunity for you to start creating your own workout DVDs to sell.

Like with the CD's however, your product needs to be ready to go, including having all your artwork and images ready.

Createspace offers guidelines to help you to deliver the best possible products. Read up on the free information and FAQ (Frequently Asked Questions) for details to help you to sell only the best products. It is one of those sites where being well prepared will really help you. If you are not well prepared, you will find yourself going back and forth during the publishing process, which will become rather frustrating.

With CreateSpace you really can develop a really great basic product base, with the added benefit of all of your products being sold directly on Amazon, the worlds' largest marketplace.

Create a multi-layered product

Your ultimate success will come in you being able to create a multi-layered product base.

What this means, is that you may not find all of your success on just one of the platforms I have mentioned in this book (and on the various other platforms I cover in my videos, visit www.patreon.com/itsmybusiness for more). You will want to be able to create a product, or a series of related products that you can launch across several platforms in several different formats.

Let me give you an example, say you create a beautiful "handmade" digital product that you are able to launch and sell on Etsy.

As you create these products, why not record a tutorial on your design process, or if it's a self assembly product, why not record a "how to" video, which you can then launch on YouTube. You can also record classes, based on your skill type, and sell these videos on Amazon through Createspace, or perhaps your lessons are effective just as audio recordings, why not sell the CDs too?

You know your trade pretty well... very well actually, why not write a book about it?

As you go along creating one or two products, you can branch out and develop it into a good few others too. Before you know it, you will have a whole host of different products, available across a wide variety of platforms. The result is, within a few years you could be earning a fairly decent passive income from a number of sources.

Remember to link up all your products. Let those who buy your books, know that you have downloadable digital products, or CDs available. Mention your online stores in the videos you record. It is possible that if a client buys one part of your product offering, that they will be willing to invest in the others, so let them know about it.

Layering for Graphic designers – a practical example

My goal here is to give you a practical example, so that you can see how easily you can translate the concept of layering to building your products to earn passive income.

Firstly I want to give you the definition for layering which pertains to the context of this book.

Layering: *Taking a single digital product or design, and selling it on a variety of platforms, in a assortment of different forms* *and formats, with a goal of earning passive income from each platform and format.*

In my book and my videos, I am mentioning and sharing this concept because it's your key to a more successful product range. To be quite honest, if you learn only one thing from me, I hope that this is it, because once you get this right and you are able to apply it, there are really just so many possibilities that open up to you.

In this example, I'm going to start with my webcomic. A few years ago, a friend and I launched this webcomic to see how much interest we could get from it. Blink and Wonky... The names come from how we would describe our internet connection if we were struggling with it for a bit. I would always say *"my internet is on the blink"* and he would *say "my internet is a bit wonky"*, and so our character's names were born.

When we first started, I used to hand sketch the comics – it was a long and tedious task. Now that my graphics skills have improved to a huge degree, I decided to "re-BOOT" the series with a new look, using digitally drawn characters. Doing this also opened a door for me to be able to create products for passive income, and the bonus part is that I actually just create these comics for fun, and a little stress relief. It's a hobby that I really enjoy.

To start, after creating a comic strip, I post the webcomic online, free for all to view. So how does this help me to earn a passive income? Firstly because it's free, I can grow my readership hassle free – and these readers knowingly or unknowingly will help me to generate an income. How so?

The first platform – Blogger
www.blogger.com / www.blogspot.com

I have been blogging on this platform for as long as I can remember, it must be at least a decade by now. Blogger is free to use, and it's a Google product, so I can easily link it up to my Google email address and Google+ without any hassle.

Because it's a Google product, it also offers me the option to earn my very first source of passive income. Blogger allows me to easily set up **AdSense ads** on my blog. Every time somebody clicks on these adverts, I get paid. It's the number one reason why I have no less than five (that's right, **5**) blogs on this platform.

In my most recent post, I introduced two furry new characters, our pet greyhounds (based on my own beloved hounds). This gave me my opportunity from this specific post.

https://blinkandwonky.blogspot.com

From the comic strip, I extracted the image of one of the greyhounds sleeping upside down. Greyhound lovers refer to this as "roaching", and it's a popular term and image on greyhound pages and sites, because let's face it, it's incredibly cute and makes our hearts laugh just a little.

The second platform – Shutterstock
www.shutterstock.com

First I'm going to sell the digital image *as is* with no background, or anything added. There's a few sites that I can sell this on, including royalty free sites such as Shutterstock. Now every time somebody purchases the vector image to use, I get paid.

I isolated the vector image of the sleeping hound, and loaded it to sell on Shutterstock. If I wanted to, I could do this with all the characters in the comic strip – even the empty "room" with the couch that they are all "standing" in. I just personally felt, that this was the only image I wanted to sell from this strip.

The third platform – Adsella
www.adsella.com

Like Shutterstock, I am just selling the vector image on Adsella. Why?

Two reasons, firstly Adsella supplies me with the html code that I can link to my webcomic, where I can sell the digital image directly to my readers. So if they like the image, they can buy it on my blog and check out via Adsella.

Secondly, to make money from other merchants. Currently there are hundreds of online stores, with more coming up every day, where people are selling t-shirts with fun and funky designs.

The concept of these stores is to "set up shop" selling fun t-shirts and sit back while the money comes in. Quite often people with these stores want to set them up quickly and easily. They invest money in a platform, and a domain name, and then put more money into online advertising, and hope to watch their new products sell. They don't necessarily have the time to make up their own designs, and so they go online and quickly purchase them from existing sources, such as Adsella and Creative Works.

You can make their lives easier, and of course earn some income for yourself, by having a few of these images already up and ready for them to buy.

But what if you want to sell your own t-shirts too but you really don't want to spend the money investing in a merchant platform and buying your own domain? After all you want to make money, not spend it.

The fourth platform – Redbubble
www.redbubble.com

I absolutely love this site. Redbubble is a market place where you can go buy really fun and funky printed goodies, from cellphone covers to t-shirts, notebooks to coffee mugs, and totes to bedding and pillows. If you really are looking for a fun gift for someone, then this is the store to buy it from.

But where does Redbubble get all of these fun designs from? Well... you! The graphic designer or artist busy sitting at home creating something new and interesting.

They have a very wide product range available – all of them blank and unprinted. When you have completed your designs, you upload them to the site and super impose them onto an assortment of products. Redbubble then sells, prints and ships the products for you, taking care of all that necessary business stuff, and you get paid your profits for doing what you do best, being an artist and designer (photographers also welcome).

Redbubble is to graphic designers, what Amazon is to authors. I think it really is one of the best platforms and opportunities that is open to us to use.

I also used this platform to launch a range of Blink and Wonky Webcomic Official Merchandise, so that fans of our comic can support us by buying branded goodies. I created the graphic on the blog, and once they click on it, it opens up to the Redbubble page where they can buy our official merch.

Platforms five to seven

So now, how can I take this one graphic, and earn even more income from it? You can create more digital products and sell these on other marketplaces.

This step takes a bit more work, but it's worth it in the end.

Here's an example, a while ago I designed a variety of stationery mock ups, which includes a variety of different gift bags, gift boxes and greeting card designs. I decided to take my sleeping greyhound, and give him a Christmas hat and a green background, making him a little more festive.

I then added this new image to a few of the stationery mock ups I have, and created a range of Christmas stationery. I saved them as digital files, ready to download and print anywhere in the world.

Adsella allows me to sell this digital stationery on their platform for their clients to buy, however I can also sell these digital products on other platforms too.

I added them to my **Etsy** store www.etsy.com, my **OurVillage** store www.ourvillage.com and my **HelloPretty** store www.hellopretty.co.za.

From just one webcomic, and a day's worth of work (but to be honest it's more fun than work really), I now have a digital product, in two different formats, selling across seven different platforms, indefinitely... and no further work is required from me, except if I wish to do a little marketing. But it really is something that I can leave now, and forget about while I go on with another project.

Once I have enough comic strips, I can look at putting together a digital comic book, which I can launch and sell through Amazon.com, but that will be some time in the future, I think.

In Conclusion

I know that I have packed a lot of information in this book, but believe it or not, this is just the top of the ice berg.

When I started down this path, I set two goals for myself.

Firstly, that I get to help at least one thousand people to start to earn their own passive income.

A part of me believes that everybody can benefit from the information I have to offer, though in reality I know that only a handful of people will really share in this opportunity to grow their knowledge, and income. It's the main reason why I wrote this book, and launched my Patreon page, to be able to reach those who would love to learn and invest in themselves - *Please feel free to share this with others that you believe will benefit from this knowledge too.*

The second goal that I set for myself, was to get to know and use no less than 100 online platforms. This way I could offer the best available information out there (and of course discover new and exciting ways of earning passive income). I have only introduced you to 22 of the platforms in this book, and there are many, many more to come.

I look forward to sharing much more information with you in the near future, until then remember that the best thing you can always do for yourself is to **invest in yourself...** and the best way to do that is through learning and growing your knowledge.

Follow me for all my latest news and updates!

Twitter: https://twitter.com/TheLife17637871

Facebook: https://web.facebook.com/lifecoachingTHELIFE

BONUS SECTION

BLOGGING
the basic money maker

how to set up an income generating blog in 5 EASY steps

by Nathalie Marran

Blogging – The Basic Money Maker
By Nathalie Marran

Index:

1. Introduction
2. My Personal Story
3. Setting Up
4. Affiliate Programs
5. Become an influencer
6. Sell your own products
7. Blog Set Up Check List

Introduction

In this section I want to share with you what can possibly your strongest foundation to starting to earn a passive income online. This is where I first started, and it's a tool that I use to this day... and that is through blogging.

I am going to show you useful practices that you can use to set up a blog and to start earning from it almost immediately.

I have touched on the subject of earning passive income from blogging briefly in my video "Cooking Up Passive Income", but I really wanted to write this so that I could delve deeper into the subject.

Suggested Reading

There are really so many books on the subject of blogging and how you can make money from it, and to be quite honest, most of them really are not even worth reading. However I do recommend reading "How to start a blog" by Lauren McManus and Alex Nerney.

They created the incredibly successful blog avocadu.com, and in their book they take you through the extremely detailed, step by step process of how they went from starting the blog to earning $10,000 dollars per month.

The book is really great for those who want to quit their day jobs and be full time bloggers.

*

Here are a few questions for you to ask yourself, answer as honestly as you can, and really think about your answers, they might just reveal a life changing realisation.

1. Is there a particular subject or hobby you really enjoy, that you can write about?

_____

_____

2. What do you really enjoy doing for fun or just to unwind and relax?

_____
_____

3. Do you want to be able to travel the world and see new places without having to worry about stopping working?

_____

4. How do you feel about retiring early and having your time to yourself? What would you do with that time?

_____
_____

5. Are there any magazines or blogs that you would like to see more of?

_____
_____

It takes roughly half an hour to write 500 words, which is a decent blog post size. Do you have 30 minutes that you can spare once a week to write a few words, which can lead to you earning passive income?

Many of the greatest minds today, including Bill Gates, believe that within a few years, poverty throughout the world can be completely eliminated through everybody learning to earn a basic income from an online source, and starting a blog is one of the easiest ways to begin to do just that.

My Personal Story

Now, you're not necessarily going to start making thousands of dollars over night, this is one of those things that will take time to get you to where you want to be. Being consistent and posting consistently will allow you to grow your blog so that it becomes an income generating base for you.

I dabbled in writing blogs since my early twenties. Before blogs were around, there were a few sites where people could sign up and write journal or diary entries online. I remember one of my friends excitedly introducing me to one of these, almost 20 years ago. I made a few posts, but I think the concept struggled to take off then as people were really wary about posting their rather personal and intimate thoughts online.

However this "online diary" approach eventually gave way to blogs, where people would write and share all kinds of things all over the internet... and it's still going quite strongly (though vlogging is also taking off exponentially, but that's another subject altogether). As long as there are people willing to write about all kinds of things, and others wanting to read them, there will always be blogs.

I tried a few platforms myself, but ultimately I decided to stick to using Blogger (www.blogger.com / www.blogspot.com) because of its ease of use.

As it stands, all these years later, I have no less than 5 blogs up and running. Wordpress is also not a bad option for the avid blogger to use (www.wordpress.com) however I find that monetising (making money from) blogger is so much easier.

Setting Up

The BIG reason why I recommend blogger over all the other sites like Wordpress and Wix is because it is FREE to start monetizing your site, where with the other platforms you have to pay upfront and go with a paid version in order to do this. As you will discover, with all the platforms I recommend to you, it's with the idea that you shouldn't have to pay anything to get started earning money.

So if you are really just looking at blogging on the side for a little extra income, then I most definitely, highly recommend using blogger.

Blogger is a Google product, and it is completely free to set up. Because it is a Google product, once you have enough readers (something that does not take long to achieve), you can choose to add a Google AdSense Account to you blog (if you do decide to go through Wordpress, then there is a plugin available to use for you, on the paid version, that allows you to link your Google AdSense account to your blog).

Google have also recently added a new rule that you have to wait 6 months to sign up to Adsense from the time you launch your blog, I imagine that this is to ensure that the blog is going to last long enough to make the advertising space worthwhile to their clients.

So how does Google Adsense work? It allows Google to place adverts on your blog, and you get paid for the advertising space. So when your readers visit your blog and see an advert they like, and click on it, you get paid.

You get paid a few cents just for the click through (Called PPC – Pay Per Click) and after a while all the cents rack up, and Google sends you money. This is the *easiest* way to begin to earn money from your blog.

Now blogs are really all about the content, and how often you post new content will depend on how successful your blog is. The more regularly you post new content, the higher your traffic flow (the amount of people who visit your blog) will be. The most successful blogs have daily posts (so that's about 30 minutes of your time writing a few 100 words, every day), but if you are doing this on the side, there's no reason why you can't do weekly posts (I don't recommend anything less often than that).

The biggest drawing card to your blog will be the QUALITY of your content, so make sure that you are writing really interesting articles that will be helpful to your readers, and of course great pictures. (Pinterest and Instagram can be your most effective marketing channels to send social media traffic your way).

When it comes to content, it can become really difficult to keep trying to figure out what to write about, well here's a way to make it really easy.

Your blog obviously has a main theme (for example one of my blogs is on Life Coaching) in order to make it easy to add new content, I have broken down my Life Coaching Brand into three subsections, and I feature each subsection on my blog, these are LIFE, MONEY and BRAND, so this gives me three different approaches to writing my content.

I recommend having between 3 to 5 subsections for your blog, but no more than that as you don't want to make your readers feel like they are being overloaded with too much information.

You then alternate between these subsections, or themes, to write content for your blog. I have a list of each subsection in my diary, and every time I think of a post to write, I place the topic under the heading. I usually try to have at least ten to twenty ideas and blog posts lined up so my readers don't get disappointed because I missed a post. Maybe once or twice a month, have a good brain storming session to come up with ideas for blog posts. If you find yourself, forcing yourself to come up with a blog post at the last minute, chances are quite high that it will be a poor quality post, which will leave you with unhappy followers.

My longest standing blog has now been going for just over eleven years, I make a habit of trying to post at least once a week, and it has 4 sub categories that attracts a variety of readers. It's one of my projects that don't take up a lot of my time, but also has dollars coming in at a steady rate.

As far as the topic of your content goes, well that part is up to you. I recommend you write about something you love and are passionate about, because your readers will be able to see that through your words. Plus, chances are that you are already involved in some social media groups with the same interests, so you already have a base group of people that you can share your posts with.

So you have your blog set up, you have fantastic content, plus your Google AdSense is set up, here are a few other ways to monetize your blog and start earning.

Affiliate Programs

Join affiliate programs. The best place to start is with Amazon.com. They have a great affiliate program, with an extremely wide variety of products to choose from. You can easily add your affiliate links and banners all across your blog to see which works best for you. Amazon gives you quite a variety of options on going about doing this.

In fact adding products from Amazon is really as easy as copying and pasting a little html code, and then sitting back and relaxing.

One of the added benefits of this is, say a day or week comes up when you just can't think of anything really great or insightful to write about, you can create a post from recommended products.

One of my favourite approaches is "My 5 top favourite *[insert products]*" so whether it's cooking implements, books on a certain topic, products related to your blog theme, etc, chances are quite high that you will find at least 5 to 10 products in the Amazon Affiliate Program that you can recommend to your readers.

Or find a book you have read, or a product you have used and write a really great review on it, add your affiliate link and share it in your post. Of course if your readers love your recommendations and click on the product to buy it, you get a nice little commission.

There are only 2 rules that you have to, have to abide by to keep your affiliate program up and running.

Rule #1: You must feature at least one free Kindle book on your blog or site
Rule #2: You must make your first affiliate associated sale within the first 180 days (6 months)

This is because Amazon wants to make sure that your "partnership" is a worthwhile and profitable one, which is only fair, and both of the above rules are very realistic.

If you are not in a major territory (that is the UK, the US, Australia, and most European countries), then Amazon may want to pay you by cheque, and you have to rack up at least $100 worth of earnings before that happens. To get past this hurdle, sign up for an account with www.Payoneer.com. They will give you an American Bank account number that Amazon can use to pay you. You get sent a bank card in the post which you will have to activate online. (CLICK HERE for a referral link from me (or type it out in your web browser) https://share.payoneer.com/nav/TqzLt_b7DnunIz9nFT2X7hxCl_Gr54QIGPmdWR2rHS1C8ckXWbXzIEZsmfOYTP4DTmC5kTyQTd48vBLzQ8XyYg2)

The first added bonus with this is that Amazon won't wait until you have racked up $100 dollars, they will pay you your money as you earn it (30 days in arrears) even if it's just a few cents. The second biggest benefit of Payoneer is that you have a card that you can swipe at any time all around the world, so no more waiting for your funds to be cleared first. (You also can earn a commission if your refer a friend to sign up for Payoneer, and they receive their first $1000 dollars into their account).

Become an influencer

So now you have two really easy ways to bring in a small amount of cash flow, though your blog, with very little work involved. So let's look at a way that involves a little more work, but is still worth it.

Become an influencer... now there's a new word that we suddenly all seem to be bombarded with. So what is an influencer? It is someone who gets sponsored and paid by companies to feature their products on their websites and blogs. The big sponsors, such as huge well known household brands usually approach extremely well known influencers directly and have contracts with them, but you are just starting out, so how can you get a piece of that influencer pie?

This is when we come to one of my favourite websites, www.fiverr.com. The name of the site comes from the fact that you pay for the services of freelancers from as low as just a "Fiverr" or $5. It is a marketing department of freelancers, and it costs nothing to get yourself set up on the site and to start marketing your own services.

My clients go to this site to place orders for me to feature their products on my blog, and for me to sell them advertising space (more on this in a bit). They pay me an amount from $5, and in return they get a blog feature as well as social media coverage for a week. It takes me only a few minutes to make the post, and to set up the social media posts to automatically go out.

As you become a more *influential* influencer (have more readers and social media followers), you will be able to increase the amount of your basic rate. I recommend going onto Fiverr.com and having a look at what other influencers are offering, as this will give you an idea of where to start and how much you can charge for your services. For example, even though my services start at $5, I charge an average of $10 per post (with a week of social media posts) – and I have a reach of around twenty thousand followers.

You can also strike up deals with bloggers and websites that have similar interests, where perhaps you can mention and advertise each others' blogs. Google LOVES this, and it increases your SEO (Search Engine Optimisation) as a result, which sends even more traffic your way.

Once you get to know your blog well enough, and if you know your way around creating graphics, you can also offer your clients the option of creating advertising space for them, and selling an "advertising banner" to them. They pay you up front (so there's no click through rates to worry about), and you feature their advertising banner according to an agreed to rate, for an agreed period of time, and link it to their website.

One of the reasons that I love Fiverr so much, is that although you may only clear $4 of the $5 charge to your clients, both you and your client are protected. Their process is simple. The client places their order and makes their payment to Fiverr. You receive the order and process it, and only once your client is happy, and the job is complete, will

Fiverr then pay you for the job. It also has a really easy to use "problem resolution centre" where if you are unhappy with your client's demands, or you can't complete an order for any reason, you can quickly and effectively cancel the order and Fiverr refunds your client.

So there you have it, the top three easiest ways for you to begin to monetize your site, and the only cost is quite literally your time.

Sell your own products

You may get to the point when you would like to create a product yourself to sell through your blog, whether it's an eBook, digital file of sorts or even a physical product. Without having to pay a web developer, or having to join a marketplace or setting up a separate online store, how can you go about selling your products through your blog?

If you are using a paid for platform such as Wordpress, or Wix, you can install a plugin that will allow you to do just that, or you can visit Gumroad (www.gumroad.com)

Gumroad has a free version that is really great for those who are looking to start selling digital products online, so how does it work?

You set up an account, link it to your PayPal account and upload your products to the site. Gumroad then generates an html code which you can embed on your blog. Once you have done that, your work is quite literally done.

When a client clicks on the item to purchase it, they will safely and securely checkout out and make payment via Gumroad, who quite literally takes care of all that back end business (for a small percentage of your sale), and then they pay you your money. They make it as easy and hassle free as possible.

This site also has an affiliate program, so if you have friends who also have blogs or websites which are suited to your products, you can send them a link of your product to feature on their site, when they make a sale, they earn a commission percentage of your choosing, and again all the back end is taken care of by Gumroad. It really cannot get easier than that.

Blog Set Up Check List

So here is your Blog set up check list to use when setting up an income generating blog:

1. Set up blog on blogger – Cost FREE (unless you want to purchase your own domain to link to it), but the blogger free domain works just as well for when you are starting up.
2. Create social media accounts – Twitter, Facebook, Instagram and Pinterest are most likely to generate your highest traffic levels, but don't be afraid to create a Google+ Page and a LinkedIn Page too.
3. Link Google AdSense and earn on advert click throughs – Cost FREE, but you will need to have a little traffic coming through your blog before Google allows you to do this (I think it's really low, something like 10 visitors), so share your shiny new blog with

friends and family to get your traffic started.
4. Sign up for an Amazon Affiliate account, and get paid to recommend products to your readers. Cost: FREE – just make note of the rules you need to follow.
5. Set up an account with Fiverr.com and become a kick ass affiliate today – Cost: FREE. You only pay your fee when a client pays you. Don't forget to add Fiverr links and icons to your blog, in case your readers want you to feature their products too.
6. Set up to sell your own digital products through Gumroad.com – Cost: FREE for the beginner package – and remember to ask your friends if they would like to join your affiliate program.

Now all that's left to do is for you to create some amazing content, and start posting. Remember to watch my marketing videos to discover FREE ways and platforms that you can use to begin to reach your target audience.

Follow me on twitter and on Facebook for more blog posts and videos to help you to **live a better life**

And remember to **Always invest in yourself**

Twitter:
https://twitter.com/TheLife17637871
Facebook:
https://web.facebook.com/lifecoachingTHELIFE/
Blog:
https://lifecoachingforthelife.blogspot.com/
Patreon:
https://www.patreon.com/itsmybusiness

www.ingramcontent.com/pod-product-compliance
Lightning Source LLC
Chambersburg PA
CBHW031420210526
45464CB00005B/1974